Brena, the Butterfly

ISBN: 978-0-578-60613-2

Printed in the United States of America

With love, I dedicate this book to Josephine and Julian.

Once upon a time, a beautiful Monarch butterfly named Brena lived in Canada. She was the oldest of three; she had a sister named Brenda, and a brother named Brandon.

Brena's mother laid her eggs on the leaves of milkweed plants. Later, the eggs went through different stages of metamorphoses: (1) larvae; (2) pupa; and (3) full adults. When the eggs hatched, they were very small caterpillars, not butterflies.

As a hungry, little caterpillar, Brena began to eat many leaves. She quickly started to grow and when she became too big for her skin, her body opened from front to back.

This is when Brena began to spin a silk thread from a small bump below her mouth to make a cocoon that would let her hang from a branch on a very large tree.

One spring day, Brena burst from her cocoon as a very colorful butterfly. She, her family, and many of their friends decided it was time to fly thousands of miles to Mexico for their yearly migration to avoid the cold winter. Young butterflies were instructed to be careful and not to stop flying so they would not be eaten by predators, such as birds, bats, frogs, lizards, flies, and wasps.

As Brena and swarms of Monarch butterflies slowly flapped their wings, children would wave at them and smile at the kaleidoscope of colors that decorated the sky.

Whenever the butterflies stopped to eat, they enjoyed a meal of nectar, tree sap, and bee honey. They were mindful not to become the prey of birds, even though most flew right past them.

To birds, the Monarchs' colorful wings meant that they wouldn't taste good. During these stops, Brena would make friends with butterflies from all over the world.

One day Brena met a very kind butterfly named Brian. They became best friends and were inseparable. Everyone was happy when Brena and Brian were married.

However, shortly after the celebration, Brena got captured by an entomologist, someone who studies insects. Brian was distraught when he found out that Brena had been taken to a laboratory for scientific research.

Fortunately, Brian was able to rescue Brena with the help of his good friends, Luke and Ralph. The couple decided to fly back to Canada and start a family. Generations of their descendants still fly to Mexico for warmer weather and live in the Monarch Butterfly Biosphere Reserve until it is time to return home.

About the Author

Jia Herring McClain was born and raised in College Park, Georgia. She is the oldest of two children and has always displayed a love of nature and science. Growing up, Jia traveled frequently due to her father's military career as well as mother's career as an airline flight attendant with a major carrier.

She believes her God-given purpose in life is to reach people across all generations and cultural backgrounds. Her mission is to educate, empower, encourage, laugh, live and love wholeheartedly. You can send your questions and comments to her at **jiamoniquewrites@gmail.com**.

Learn More About Monarch Butterflies

https://www.monarch-butterfly.com

https://www.nationalgeographic.com/animals/invertebrates/m/monarch-butterfly/

https://www.travelandleisure.com/travel-news/monarch-butterfly-migration-mexico

Made in the USA
Columbia, SC
06 January 2020